MEMORIES OF THE BEACH

MEMORIES OF THE BEACH

Reflections on a Toronto Childhood

Lorraine O'Donnell Williams

DUNDURN PRESS
TORONTO

Editor: Shannon Whibbs
Design: Courtney Horner
Printer: Webcom

Library and Archives Canada Cataloguing in Publication

Williams, Lorraine O'Donnell, 1932-
      Memories of the Beach : reflections on a Toronto
childhood / by Lorraine O'Donnell Williams.

ISBN 978-1-55488-389-9

      1. Williams, Lorraine O'Donnell, 1932- --Childhood
and youth. 2. Beaches, The (Toronto, Ont.)--Biography.
3. Beaches, The (Toronto, Ont.)--History. 4. Toronto
(Ont.)--Biography. 5. Toronto (Ont.)--History. I. Title.

FC3097.26.W54A3 2010   971.3'54103092   C2009-907461-3

1 2 3 4 5   14 13 12 11 10

 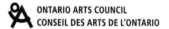

We acknowledge the support of the **Canada Council for the Arts** and the **Ontario Arts Council** for our publishing program. We also acknowledge the financial support of the **Government of Canada** through the **Canada Book Fund** and **The Association for the Export of Canadian Books**, and the **Government of Ontario** through the **Ontario Book Publishers Tax Credit program**, and the **Ontario Media Development Corporation**.

Photograph on page 3 (l–r): Bill Williams, Velma Williams, Irma Glynn, Nina Cressy, Florence Byrnes, Frank Byrnes.

J. Kirk Howard, President

Published by The Dundurn Group
Printed and bound in Canada.
www.dundurn.com

Unless otherwise indicated, all photos are credited to the author's private collection.

Dundurn Press	Gazelle Book Services Limited	Dundurn Press
3 Church Street, Suite 500	White Cross Mills	2250 Military Road
Toronto, Ontario, Canada	High Town, Lancaster, England	Tonawanda, NY
M5E 1M2	LA1 4XS	U.S.A. 14150

Mixed Sources
Product group from well-managed
forests, and other controlled sources
www.fsc.org Cert no. SW-COC-002358
© 1996 Forest Stewardship Council
FSC

Contents

To my mother and father, who gave me the gift of life to live *this* life, and to my dear husband John and our children, Theresa, Megan, Harland, Maureen, and Barbara, who have made life so fulfilling.

> *It's by remaining faithful to the contingencies and peculiarities of your own experience and the vagaries of your own nature that you stand the greatest chance of conveying something universal.*
> — David Shields, "Reality, Persona" in *Truth in Nonfiction*, edited by David Lazar

Preface ———————————)

*L*ike most writers, I keep stacks of clippings from newspapers, magazines, and other media stashed haphazardly in nominal files. However, an old clip I came across recently left me with a question: "Modern life fills children with anxiety, study finds" (*National Post*, December 15, 2000). It went on to describe a massive study of five decades, which concluded, "The slow disintegration of the ties that bind society together is creating generations of chronic worriers."

It was then that I realized that the memoirs I was writing — about growing up in the 1930s and 1940s — were filled with some incidents of anxieties, but the overall tone was one of security interspersed with challenge. And certainly, the anxiety never led to me developing into a chronic worrier. Quite the opposite. I tend to be more in the "things always turn out for the best" school. Then I began to muse: was it possible that my childhood days marked the last, or near last, "age of innocence"?

Unwilling to be accused of being a Pollyanna, a non-realist, an idealist, I took a critical eye to the events of my upbringing. I knew that the decade in which I was born had not been free of stress and pain. It was the decade when Charles and Anne Lindbergh's twenty-month-old son was kidnapped and later found murdered; when millions of North Americans were out of work due to the Great Depression; when Joseph

Stalin's wife was suspected of committing suicide; when the Second World War broke out. But good things were happening, as well. New York's Radio City Music Hall opened. The Toronto Maple Leafs won the Stanley Cup. If you had any money, the price of a house averaged six thousand dollars and a loaf of bread cost a mere seven cents. A new car cost $610 and gas was ten cents a gallon. Elizabeth Taylor was born!

Reviewing my growing-up years over those two decades and comparing them to the society in which my children and their children will have to live, I have an increased understanding of how difficult it is for today's generation to discern how to make positive choices. The growing prosperity after the war years, plus societal changes wrought by the war, were a prelude to the revolutionary social mores of the 1960s. Individualism and relativism are now dominant. Guidelines are often fuzzy or non-existent. By learning about times that were different, this generation may be encouraged to know that life was and can be different. That it's possible to restore some of that innocence into their world.

I realize my life had an extra dimension that coloured it forever. Growing up at the Beach (or the Beaches, as many Torontonians refer to it) infused my nature with a resiliency as multi-faceted as the moods of Lake Ontario, and a foundation as firm as the grand old willow trees that line the boardwalk. I was truly blessed, as was every child who was a son or daughter of the Beach.

Bring back "the old days"? No, that's not possible or even desirable. But honour those old days? Yes — and realize there are ways to integrate their values into today's anxious world.

Introduction
Growing Up on the Boardwalk

Every man has within himself the entire human condition.
— David Shields, "Reality, Persona" in *Truth in Nonfiction*

Today *The Beach neighbourhood is considered a safe stable place for busy Torontonians to live and raise a family.* It is a trendy oasis of relaxation, and a refuge from the summer humidity that can wither city dwellers. But in 1793 when the Ashbridge family started to farm there, it was boggy, buggy, and plain hard work. The family, who'd moved there from Philadelphia in 1793 when John Graves Simcoe was lieutenant-governor, was determined to persevere in civilizing this lakefront wasteland. By the 1850s, other pioneers had joined them, including a settler named Joseph Williams. Williams bought a farm near the present-day Queen Street and Lee Avenue area and named it Kew Farms. Ever a man of enterprise, he designated a sector of it as The Canadian Kew Gardens. Contemporary documents described it as "a pretty pleasure ground of twenty acres, fifteen in bush, fronting on the open lake." It offered "innocent amusements in great variety, including dancing," and "temperate drinks, but no Spirituous Liquors." The resourceful Williams instead sold his own milk and buttermilk as "the temperate drinks."

The Beach area grew as the public became increasingly interested in its developing attractions. In 1876, a new subdivision between Silver Birch and Balsam Avenues reserved a "private promenade" on the waterfront for lot buyers. Streetcar and steamer service became available. The Toronto Gravel and Concrete Company built a tramway along the south side of Kingston Road. Horse-drawn trams brought picnickers to Woodbine Park (site of the first Woodbine Rack Track). New streets laid out in Balmy Beach Park bore the name of trees. (Veteran Beachers to this day maintain if you didn't live on a street named after a tree you weren't really a son or daughter of the Beach.) Still, life was not entirely civilized. People who went to work on winter mornings to downtown Toronto had to have a lantern which they left in a little shed at Woodbine Avenue. When they returned at night, they'd pick up their lantern, light it, and walk home.

Thomas O'Connor, a Catholic layman and benefactor of the Sisters of St. Joseph, was another Torontonian who owned a huge block of lakefront land. He bequeathed his farm, consisting of forty acres of land and twenty-four acres of water lots stretching from the lake to Queen Street East, from Leuty to MacLean Avenues to the St. Joseph congregation. After his death in 1895, the Sisters farmed the area as a profitable dairy and garden produce source. They used the income to maintain one of their major projects in the city — the House of Providence on Power Street, a huge institution for the indigent, sick, and aged. Finally, in 1906 the Sisters decided to sell the fertile farm site and establish a new farm on St. Clair Avenue East.

In a short-sighted decision, Toronto City Council declined to buy it because they considered it too expensive. The Sisters sold the property to Harry and Mabel Dorsey in 1908 for the sum of $165,000. By

House of Providence, Power Street looking north to St. Paul's Basilica. Food for the city's indigents was supplied by its huge dairy and produce farm on the future site of the Scarboro Beach Amusement Park.

Gordon H. Jarrett.

1927 Aerial view of Scarboro Beach Amusement Park. It was a drawing card for thousands to the Beach every summer.

that time this eastern section had a population of about 5,000. It was developing into a year-round settlement with a school and churches. This growth was initially the result of the Toronto Railway Company's expansion of service. It had installed streetcar tracks along Queen to Balsam in 1891 — for summer use only. Then, in 1901 East Toronto was incorporated into the City proper. By 1900 a third of the 287 lakefront homes east of Woodbine were no longer merely summer cottage escapes, but were occupied on a permanent basis. Queen Street was gradually extended past the R.C. Harris Water Treatment Plant (known to locals as the Water Works and site of an illegal driving range to many aspiring young golfers). They had no inkling that in future years it would be celebrated in Michael Ondaatje's novel, *In the Skin of a Lion*. Queen East ended at Fallingbrook Avenue and the Hundred Steps, at whose base was a small dance pavilion. The Dorseys recognized the land's potential. There'd already been a series of short-lived amusement parks at different locales along the lake. They had a vision of an amuse-

ment park on the site patterned after New York's Dreamland. They
invested $600,000 to build the largest park with the most attractions
ever put in the Beach area. In March of that year, a contest was held to
choose a name for it. It opened June 1, 1907 as Scarboro Beach Park. It
had everything that Coney Island ever had! There was a bandstand and
a scenic railway that took visitors all around the grounds. the Shoot the
Chutes ride had an opening underneath the spectators' walkway for the
boats. There was a multitude of choices — the Whirl of Pleasure, the Di-
sasters Presentations, and the Electroscope, a bathhouse, the Scarboro
Inn restaurant, and a carousel. Amidst the other hundred attractions
the extremely long roller coaster ride proved popular, as did the Bump
the Bumps Slide, Shoot the Chutes, and the Tunnel of Love. Performers
used the thirty-eight-metre-high tower for daredevil acts. A miniature
steamship train transported merrymakers all around the grounds. At
night, thousands of lights decorated the park. Families would gather in
their canoes and rowboats at the lakeshore to listen to concerts. Pro-
fessional lacrosse (officially designated as Canada's sole national game
until 1994) and other sports were played at the athletic grounds, which
featured a wooden velodrome. That interest in sports was to remain
constant, with the Beach being the home of many softball, water sports,
and tennis championship teams through the decades. The first public
exhibition flights in Canada were made there by Charles Willard in
September 1909. After almost two glorious decades, the amusement
park closed on September 12, 1925.

The City had not been idle during this time. After the Dorsey pur-
chase and the subsequent success of its amusement park, it started accu-
mulating other parcels of land on the lake, including the grounds and ad-
joining properties of Joseph Williams and designated it as Toronto Parks'
own Kew Gardens. Eventually all of the waterfront lands from Woodbine
Avenue to Balsam were transformed into well-manicured green parks
with plenty of recreational facilities fronted by a three-and-a-half-kilo-
metre boardwalk. The park area, known as Kew Beach Park and Balmy
Beach Park was eventually divided into four — Woodbine, Kew Beach,
Scarboro Beach, and Balmy.

There was one city-owned exception to the designation of all this
acreage as parkland. There was a short block on the south side of Hub-

Beach residents were full of pride in 1939 when King George VI and Queen Elizabeth officiated at the King's Plate run at the Woodbine Race Track.

bard Boulevard. It ran along the boardwalk west from the bottom of Wineva Avenue to the bottom of Hammersmith. It was called Hubbard Boulevard and it was in the house at number 13 where I spent my childhood. Our house was built on the site of that amusement park which had been a place of happiness for so many thousands.

Sometime after the seventies, the area, always known as the Beach, began to be referred to as the Beaches. For a couple of decades, residents argued as to the proper designation. Finally, a plebiscite by residents in the spring of 2006 decided the issue. On April 18 it was announced that the traditional name, the Beach, had won. Now it was official.

This memoir is a celebration of the Beach and its role in my life and the lives of ordinary Beach people who were moving from the Depression through the Second World War to peacetime. It is difficult to write about those times and places without indulging in sentimentality. Yet that such a contained area could produce the likes of Glenn Gould, Doris McCarthy, Norman Jewison, Robert Fulford, Jack Kent Cooke, Ted Reeves, Bruce Kidd, and other contributors to the Canadian fabric surely points to that "something special about the Beach" that is oft cited by former residents. There are hundreds of others not mentioned specifically here with whom I interacted. This is a celebration of their lives, as well.

It is my hope that this description of the intersection of a unique setting, a mixed historical era, and one family's story will show how the places in which we are nurtured influence the people we become. The details may be personal, but the implications are universal.

Chapter 1

Floating

"Till then, feed on innocent bubble air, enjoy your little life, and make your mother happy."
— Sophocles, *Ajax*

I'm a water baby, floating lazily with my back to the pebbly lake bottom, full of wonder at the bubbles rising and the flashes of coloured light that break around me. The water is warm, soothing, wrapping me like a cradle as I rock back and forth with the rhythm of the waves. Time is measured by streams of bubbles languidly moving toward a sun that is almost too brilliant for my eyes to bear. I feel a sense of perfect peace. I am drowning …

If you're born a son of the Beach (as we later daringly labelled ourselves), you know Lake Ontario intimately. When I was two years old, I almost came to know it too intimately when it tried to claim me. My mother was sitting on the sand with her friend Ev and Joyce, Ev's daughter. Whatever it was they were talking about distracted my mother, because when she looked out she couldn't see me. In panic, she raced across the broad

My mother, who always had a sense of style, prided herself on getting the best tan on the beach.

stretch of sand to the shore. She spotted me, and my bubble-air reverie was violently interrupted, as she snatched me by my flimsy sunsuit and clasped me to her breast.

The miracle was that her panic didn't stay with me. Forever, water will be only a source of solace and serenity to me. If my life should end by drowning, I will embrace my executioner as an old friend, reclaiming me to peace.

———————

I grew up in a time when everyone knew how things should happen, even though sometimes things didn't turn out that way. It was a time when couples got married for life, had their children after that, and lived lives of laughter, high spirits — and spirit — and made sacrifices for their family or their country because their parents has taught them that was what we were here for.

Where did my life begin? In my mother Velma's womb, the fruit of her passionate love for Neil, the bright, fun-loving, youngest-of-eight-boys who was the love of her life. I'd beg her to tell me that story of their first meeting over and over again: "I was at Balmy Beach Canoe Club standing with my girlfriend Phyllis on one side of the hall. It was a dance. Your father was across the room with some other fellows. I watched him for a long time, then I turned to Phyll and said 'That's the man I'm going to marry.'"

The club had been a focus for Beach activity since 1903, and became so popular that its small boathouse had to be replaced by a larger clubhouse in 1905. Balmy athletes were well known. As early as 1924 they had won gold and four bronze medals for sprint canoe in the Paris Olympic Games. They continued to garner awards, including several at the national level. Balmy's football team won Canada's Grey Cup in 1927 and 1930. Fire destroyed the clubhouse in 1936 and again in 1963. The present clubhouse was reopened in 1965. But, for my parents and their friends, it was a social centre, an inexpensive place to have fun in dark economic times when, according to my mother's girlfriend Phyllis, "we ate a lot of sausages, carrots, and tapioca pudding because they were the cheapest."

In the full fury of the Great Depression, 1931 was a daring time to marry. Most businesses demanded that if a woman married, she had to forfeit her job. Dad was following in the footsteps of his older brothers — all of them salesman who surely in some prior life had kissed the Blarney Stone. Selling was in his blood as deeply as his Irish love of rum. When he announced his engagement, his older brother and mentor Arnold was not impressed. "You don't have any money to get married on." Undeterred, these true devotees of the flapper generation were wed by Father

McGrath in a simple ceremony in Corpus Christi Church at Lockwood and Queen East. In 1931, the church, now designated as a heritage property and containing a little-publicized treasure — namely a three-themed mural by famed Canadian-Ukranian artist William Kurelek — was in its second incarnation, having been expanded in 1927 to accommodate the growing Catholic population of the Beach. Velma and Neil then went on a quickie weekend honeymoon to Buffalo, financed by Arnold's generous gift of fifty dollars. This was the same uncle who confessed to me when I was a married woman, "You know, when Neilly brought your mom to my house to meet me, I thought she was a funny-looking little thing." His expression obviously equated "funny" with "homely." I wondered if he'd noticed the marks on my mother's cheeks, spaced like seed pits of a strawberry, but devoid of colour. The ones I used to dare to trace with my fingers and count, enjoying the sensation of being that close to her. "I caught scarlet fever when I was young. I almost died from it. That's how I got all these marks on my skin," she'd explain.

Uncle Arnold would reminisce some more. "I tried to talk your dad out of marriage, but he said he figured two could live cheaper than one. I never knew how he did arrive at that one (chuckle, chuckle). But you know, it did turn out okay after all."

I arrived a year and a day after their marriage, the same year that the Toronto Maple Leafs won the Stanley Cup. My parents brought me from St. Mike's Hospital to their one-bedroom basement apartment in Howell Manor, at the southwest corner of Queen and Beech. From the building's front door, you could look south several hundred yards and see the lake. That beautiful backdrop of water was to act as my lifelong touchstone.

One of my first memories was a ceremony of approval. I'd just turned three. My father had given my mother a Silex coffeepot for Christmas, the kind with a glass rod joining the upper and lower sections. In the excitement, the rod got lost somewhere among the crumpled wrapping paper. The search was on! Persistently scrunching up every scrap of tissue, I finally found it and proudly held it out to my father. Taking it from me, he announced in a proud tone, "Now, isn't she smart, Velma?" I was labelled for life.

My mother didn't have much first-hand experience with mothering. From the time she started school until she finally quit at the age of